Long Distance Home...

Rajarshi Choudhury

BookLeaf Publishing

India | USA | UK

to

all the

love and life

that comes

again and again

before

I am ready

for it;

it is this,

that becomes

poetry

Acknowledgements

I want to honour everyone, everything that has touched my life up to this moment – the joys and the sorrows, the people I have liked and loved, those I have disliked and even despised. Every experience, every encounter, has its place, each link connected in a long, unbroken chain that has shaped the person I am today. To the laughter and the heartbreak, to the friends and the adversaries, to the fleeting moments and lasting memories – I am grateful. For it is in these twists and turns, in the highs and the lows, that my story has been written.

And in acknowledging it all, I embrace not just who I am, but every fragment that has brought me here.

Preface

Musing on – Life, love, longing & just time pass…

Ah, but isn't it remarkable? Language, with all its inevitable limitations, is still the finest companion to the desperate longing of our abandoned hearts. Even in its inadequacy, language holds an unmatched beauty, an elegance that even our most delicate emotions lean into when all else fails. Poetry, of all language's offerings, stands unparalleled in this regard.

Poetry, my friend, is my soul's whispered confession, the rarest alchemy, where my thoughts and feelings intertwine in a delicate dance, transforming mere words into something transcendent. Poetry awakens me, stirs my soul with the grace of an ancient rite, listens to me without needing anything from that act, holds me without harm, dances with my shadows as if they were light, is a timeless haven, a mirror of my unspeakable truths, wrapping around me like the most tender of embraces. In its arms, I find a realm beyond language itself – a space where silence speaks and the heart is unmasked, raw and beautiful.

In this collection of poems, I have sought to unravel a question both timeless and elusive: How far am I willing to travel in search of home? And what does 'home' even mean? Is it just the roof over my head, a specific place, a goal or a destination? And yet, there lies a deeper possibility: perhaps this home I seek is an internal sanctuary, where I retreat to find peace and feel whole?

This journey, whether it leads me inward or outward, compels me to confront an even more profound question: What are the true elements of this home? For no home is merely brick and mortar, no shelter formed only by walls and roofs. The essence that transforms any dwelling into a true home is love. Love is the sacred substance that breathes life into empty rooms, that whispers a sense of belonging into every corner, creating a sanctuary that calls to my deep inner core. And belonging – ah, it is the magnetic force, that undeniable pull, which draws me closer. For at my core, I long to belong. I am a seeker of places where I feel whole, where I am cherished, where love abides.

In this seeking, I am led through the labyrinth of human experience. I may search for belonging in the eyes and embrace of another, in those moments of intimacy where I hope to find fragments of home. At times, I delve into the depths of my own existence, searching for the comfort of self-acceptance. Sometimes, I wander the vast, abiding loneliness of my own soul, hoping to stumble upon familiarity in its quiet shadows. And at other times, I linger in memories, revisiting those distant shores where I once felt whole. Each poem in this collection is a step in that journey, a search for what it means to truly find home.

Looking out in the dark
For the flowers in my heart

I struggled through this process, pouring everything I had into it, sometimes feeling like I was bleeding dry, picking up the scattered pieces of my own broken heart as I went along. But somehow, in the depths of that pain, I caught a glimmer – a silver lining. I began to see that there's a secret woven into all: only a heart that has known breaking can truly hold the depths of love. Only a heart that's been shattered open can know love that's pure and boundless, love without shadows, love that doesn't demand or possess. For when my heart is broken, it makes space – space for everyone and everything, without limits.

And so, if you're truly seeking love, if you long to love and be loved in this deeper way, be prepared to have your heart broken – not just once, but again and again. It's in those breaks that love finds room to grow, expanding into something far beyond what an unbroken heart could ever hold.

Most of these poems are intimate conversations with the self – quiet exchanges where thoughts drift and settle, unravelling the inner landscape piece by piece. They touch on themes of love, life, pain, loss, identity and the ceaseless search for meaning. Sometimes, these musings take on a cyclic rhythm that, I'll admit, can get a bit repetitive. I spend much of my life in my head, carrying on intimate, ongoing dialogues with my experiences, my perceptions and my own understanding of life. Many of these poems are attempts to capture those conversations I have with myself, the internal reflections that shape my perspective.

And then there is love – that paradoxical force, at once a giver and a plunderer. It is the beginning and the end and everything that fills the spaces in between. Love is what makes life worthwhile, what gives meaning to the ordinary and somehow makes suffering bearable. It's a force that I search for in others, only to discover, in some mysterious way, that it has always lived within me. Yet to truly know this love within myself, I need to see its reflection in someone else's eyes. Only then does it feel real – complete, as if it's been waiting to be recognised all along.

What a grievous injustice we commit against ourselves, shackling love to a single soul, as if the heart were a vessel too small to hold more than one tide. Love, in its truest form, is vast, infinite – a current meant to flow freely, not be damned by the narrow confines of convention. Yet, we carve it into cages, mistaking possession for devotion, mistaking exclusivity for depth. And in doing so, we do not honour love – we diminish it, reducing its wild, radiant expanse to a mere whisper of what it was meant to be. In truth, my heart thrives on a far grander maxim: to love as deeply and widely as it can. Only by opening myself to this abundance do I truly become whole, expanding my heart to carry a piece of the universal soul within me. To love fully, without bounds, is to embrace all that I am – to step into the richness of human potential and allow love to flow through me, reaching everyone it touches. In this limitless embrace, I find not only myself but a connection to something far greater, a reminder that love was never meant to be rationed. When I have the courage to open myself to the fullness and abundance of love then – it floods in, unbidden, wrapping itself around my life with an almost ferocious generosity; it sweeps me up whole, and in that overwhelming tide, I find myself both filled and emptied.

Like every rose, love also has its thorns. With the beauty of love comes the sting of loss, the ache of despair, for of all forms of abandonment, the loss of love is the most profound. To love is to risk, to open oneself to both the heights of joy and the depths of sorrow. So, when one sings of love, one inevitably sings of pain, of abandonment, of the empty spaces love leaves behind when it's gone. To accept love's richness is to be willing to receive all that it offers – the joy, the ache, the rapture and the loss – without holding back. Love demands this surrender, this willingness to be reshaped by its touch, to let it become part of our very fabric. And it is here, in this unguarded exchange, in all its abundance, that love becomes poetry.

In these poems, love and loss move together, entwined – one unable to exist without the shadow of the other. Because, to capture love in its entirety, I must also acknowledge the wounds it left behind. Through these poems, I aim to capture the complex, often bittersweet essence of love and the profound transformation it has woven into the fabric of my being. Each touch, each moment – whether joyful or painful – has left its mark, reshaping who I am, forever altering the landscape within me.

Long Distance Home...

Looking into
the distant past
my eyes gather shadows of sights
fragments of forgotten light
spectres of memories
that are difficult to remember
as I grow old
the more gravity diminishes
the more I slip through time in silence
Love stays on
but not the lovers
I remain – a wanderer,
forever in search of home.

Where am I now?
How far from the place I belong?
How far away from home?
Where am I?

Searching desperately for a navigator
to find my way home
Long distant home

it must be somewhere
in the violet of the lilacs
in the blood of the soil
in the fear of the dust
in the fire, which makes oceans exist
there is something wild about the thoughts
that turn into dreams
really wild
something wild about going
in search of destiny
something wild in the dare
that make us dream

We are made of stories,
stitched from longing and rapture,
with a quiet ache to return to the beginning,
to the place where we were whole,
so I keep searching and
chasing the echoes of home
as the winds from home touch my face
I tremble
I let these winds sculpt my eyes
define my vision
the winds make me quiver inside
and time, as if it has stopped

slowly I traverse time
passing through all the light
announcing the arrival
of myself
I am rooted in motion
I am rooted in illusion

there is no I
there is no us
only triangles, rounds and lines
and our pulse, tissues and muscles know this
by heart
it is engraved deeper in our bodies
the truth breaths within
there is no time but just the moment; now
and in that
now
there are endless moments
there are so many doors to enter
oneself ...pass through the myriad I
wipe the rosary of fears of the child within
one by one, with care
renew the child pulsating in the intimate
rhythm of our cells

no shadows pursue me now,
no horizons call my name, anymore
I have ceased to wander for the path has
become me
I am home,
in the breath between worlds
in the stillness beneath motion
not bound by place,
not cradled by the folds and fades of time
the winds murmur forgotten truths,
stars bleed their light into my veins,
and I dissolve–
of what remains is a whisper
an echo of
the eternal.
Here, I am.
Here, I am nothing.
Here, I am all.

Rebirth...

Here I am again.
a winter afternoon, quiet
the sun filters through, pale and empty
it's just... there.
Silent. Watching.
cold seeps in everywhere–
within
and
without.

I tread lightly, unsure,
as if walking a thread spun
from my own uncertainty.
inside, a lunatic dances, wild and restless,

throwing open doors to faces I thought I'd
forgotten
but etched in shadows and light
they've always been there
rooted inside me
they rise, these echoes of me
a chorus of voices
jumbled in their insistence to
be heard
they speak in tongues I barely remember
they speak – loud, soft, all at once
a cacophony of questions, doubts, fears

I sit with them, these pieces of myself,
trying to arrange their cacophony into
silence.
arranging, rearranging,
like maybe this time it'll all fit
but it never does
and silence doesn't come easy,
it's a knot, tight and unfathomable,
and I am caught in its tangles–
a stranger in the labyrinth of
my own emotions.

And then I realise – I'm not just hearing
them.
I'm inside them
inside this... knot of emotions,
too tight to untangle.
like you've met yourself,
but not the self you were hoping for
so many versions of me,
so many feelings
so many faces, so many tongues,
each one speaking truth I barely recognise
I met myself in this chaos,
and there are no words–
none that fit, none that feel true.

There's dust settling on my face
clouds hovering over my head
shadows draped in every corner–
long, tilted, unmoving
everything still, everything feels tangled:
memories, fears, questions, threads crossing
and knotting endlessly.

Some part of this has
to stay

it belongs to the stillness,
to the weight of all
that's unresolved,
but the rest? It moves.
I whisper to myself,
life is motion
even in stillness, it flows.

So I close my eyes,
not to escape,
but to listen
not to the noise,
but listen to...
what's between the noise.
the spaces between the sound
the silence–

And there, in the quiet,
I find my breath again.
soft and steady,
reminding the body how to be.
Breathe. Breathe. Breathe. Breathe.
Slowly.
There's something ancient about the breath,
the way it knows its rhythm

even when everything else is chaos
inhale, exhale, slowly
the body remembers to breath
even when I forget
my mind begins to trust again
in life

The steps don't feel certain,
but they're there,
moving through unwritten places,
towards something undefined
doubts linger, but they're anchors now,
not weights.

And there's a pause–
just long enough to notice.
The moment holds itself still,
fragile but real.
Breath flows in,
breath flows out.
fear softens in its rhythm.
emptiness shifts,
becoming less a void,
more a space
made of Stillness

In that stillness,
the sun begins to rise again,
its light, faint but steady,
grows,
this is what remains,
this quiet, this warmth,
this slow rebirth.

Nowhere Song

Nowhere man, singing his nowhere song,
Twisted melodies turning right into wrong.
A hollow tune with no refrain,
Carved from shadows of love and pain.

The nowhere song speaks without a voice,
A silent hymn where hearts rejoice.
Bleeding softly, it keeps you sane,
A tender dissolve beyond the pain.
No judgement lingers, no rules confine,
Just a fleeting echo outside of time.
A song that fills the hollow spaces,
Whispering truths beyond the races.

It spins and spirals, a dance unending,
A path that curves without pretending.
Round and round, it seeks no end,
A fragile loop that cannot mend.

Beneath an icy, opaque sky,
Where dreams dissolve and echoes die,

The silence grows; it swallows whole,
Devour the corners of your soul.

When breath betrays, and tears collide,
You break apart, yet still survive.
For to be human is to hope and try,
To rise again when you long to die.

The nowhere song has no meaning clear,
No victory waits, no answers near
It's in the trying, in the ache of being,
The secret of life lies unseen.

Nowhere man, I hear your song,
It echoes where my heart belongs.
Through love I've lost and pain I've known,
Your lonely tune feels like my own.

falling in love

as lovers we betrayed each other
and gambled time in exchange

you changed your smile
in marijuana miasma and
I soaked life in whisky to
reign over alcoholic nights in
desperate isolation

disoriented by shades of delusion
we descended into a dream which
ended in the lunacy of
reality
what a waste of life it was
falling in love

We

A veil of enigma,
shrouded in darkness,
enfolds my Sunday mornings,
where time lingers,
unhurried,
as I wrestle
with the shadows
of my past nights.

I sift through old letters,
each stained with traces of you
some drops of blood,
and endless longing
a spirit that dares
to traverse the chasms
of deep, aching despair.
Is that not something?

In these ruins,
raw passion plays
with a profound lack of wisdom.
we lost our glorious laughter,
exchanging whispered promises
for hollow words, which helped us
clung to the delusion
that we were anything
but ordinary–
dancing beneath the banyan tree,
its branches cradling our dreams,
we danced among the leaves,
green waves enveloping us,
yet in the end,
we became shadows
of ourselves,
chasing only flickers of sunshine,
trying to grasp moments
that slipped
through our fingers

But oh, in that moment–
time stood still–
absolutely still,

the moment we uttered
our final farewell.
pretence shattered like glasses,
the night swallowed us whole,
the silence thundered,
and the word
'we'
vanished between us,
as if it belonged
to a distant century,
a life not lived,
to another you,
to some other me.

Silences

I.
In the end,
what did you truly live for?
Was it a sadness
that clung only to your bones,
or did you bear the weight
of a grief that seeped
into the veins of humanity?

Were you part of a generation
lost in shadows,
haunted by the echo
of desperate dreams,
trying to convince yourself
that all is not lost,
yet?
Did you surrender to fear,
or did you lay down your life
for love that with time had
slipped through your fingers
like cigarette smoke?

We all meet our end,
searching for a refuge within,
a place where desire and memory
coil around our hearts,
concealed in the dampness
of high grass,
as we stare at the sky, ever-changing
time tearing us apart,
the once vibrant chambers
where our voices dared to soar
now muffled
by the relentless passage
of days and nights.

Let us not drift quietly
into the night,
but linger
as much as we can
in the shadows,
searching for remnants
of the love we lost,
for the voices that ache
to be heard once more,
even if they tremble,
even if they fade.

Can you feel it?
The deeper silence breathing
within you–
that profound silence
the silence that I am,
the silence that you are,
a vast expanse of being,
that effaces
everything fleeting,
leaving behind only echoes
of what shall transcend
time.

2.

Where destiny promised
we would meet,
a lifetime has withered,
wandering those empty streets.
Flesh and blood,
consumed by love and grief,
burned into ash.
Only the taste lingers,
as a faint trace

in nebulous memories

The art,
the beauty,
the ornaments of our time–
all gone.

it quietly rains now
as the night descends
the whole of creation
resolved to silence...

October

Pale, she returned
  from the brink of death,
  then slowly with time,
  love began to heal,
  as love so often does...

The only sounds of life
  for her were the steady beeps of the
machines,
  while he lingered alone
  in the hospital lounge,
With passing time
  they discovered
  that we endure
life for love,
  and we endure love

only because we are lonely
terribly terribly
lonely deep inside...

With every struggle, they realised
more certainly that
the love we feel
for one another reflects the love
we all carry within ourselves.
It is only through loving others
that we truly acknowledge this love
deep within ourselves

As days turned into months,
waiting lost its meaning.
Yet in the heart of his heart,
his faith remained unshakable.
but living with faith
as your only hope
is the most dismal
of all realities

By the end,
he was convinced that

only for him
she would go on living
amongst altering forms
to keep holding him
         in her warmth
and keep him glowing
         with life...

Ode to the Ordinary

Ode to the ordinary
the everyday
the common
all the things that everyone owns
and no one desires

ode to the things
that make us human
to all the things good
but not good enough
they become the everyday

Ode to the ordinary,
who exist because they must,
giggling in half-hearted gossips,
recalling who said what,
but when the truth is asked of them,
their lips seal in silence.

ode to the ordinary
whose morality flickers
as they sell their soul

for fleeting pleasures
a drink, a high, a fuck
a promise that fades with the dawn.
ode to the
drunken, jobless, homeless,
the non-productive
who let their days slip away,
dying a little every day,
in every corner of the world

ode to the ordinary
who live in sperms and die in them too
a strange similarity binds them
in life and death
ode to the ordinary
who all look the same
want the same
live the same
wherever they are
however wide in space and time

ode to the ordinary
who die in wars, tsunamis, mill strikes
or just for the want of a blanket
whose search for fortune

ends in the assurance of death
their dreams left dangling
on walls of unfulfilled hope,
slipping slowly into the abyss of time.

ode to the ordinary
who stand in the background
and only values things which others have
they sleep with hands on their heart
dreaming of all that could go wrong once they
wake up
ode to the ordinary
whose whole life spent waiting for
better days

Ode to the ordinary,
who search everywhere
for meaning,
but never look within
who have no enemies
nor friends
living lonesome amongst their families
ode to the ordinary
who were there in the beginning,
and will be there in the end,

silent witnesses,
waiting

ode to the ordinary
in whose heart hemlock simmer
as they curse the light and are blinded
by the glittering darkness
who despises the different
and then repent in silence for
ages uncounted

ode to the ordinary
Who never sees the fire in their own soul
while they celebrate others
it is their hope which creates heroes
ode to the deathless
who will be there forever
making others shine

Unforgettable...

She made love to both of us at once—
unforgettable love,
beneath a sky tangled with antennas and
electric wires—
an unforgettable love.

Rain fell outside the empty windows,
a relentless rain, washing all else away,
yet leaving behind
an inextinguishable pain
It moved through
memories and boredom,
up and down,
like the rhythm of lost time.

She made love in dark beds, exquisitely slow,
under the dim flicker of a candle.
An intelligent woman, a beautiful woman–
tired, so tired!
of the years of wars
she waged within herself.

We are all utterly desperate,
tranquil in our loneliness,
sitting on bathroom floors,
smoking through endless nights
as the rain chattered outside.
She had nowhere to go–
neither did I.
Maybe we'd wander through coffee shops,
circle cold, empty streets,
trying to remember the nice things that once
happened
childhood memories, parents' love,
all the chances lost
and the words we no longer have the courage
to say.

We searched, frantically,
for the life that remains even in ashes,
for the quiet longings we carry in our bones
for what remains after all the goodbyes
the lingering echoes of
the majesty and the misery,
of being in love.

Apple

to imagine her
you need to see things beyond
walk away from everything
if you want to walk in
a dialogue with the invisible
must be entwined in your routine
when curious is your thinking
she descends in your dreams
unchained, unbound, there is no fixed
pattern
a bodiless shadow invisible to the collective
eye
to ascertain her secrets, best of minds try
once she bares her disguise, it's all so simple
all Newton saw was a swooping apple
And the universe
revealed itself in his gaze.

Rumblings of a Cityite

How much does the City of Joy drink each
night?
How many silent tears and whispered pains
spill into its hidden cracks,
far from the crowded lights,
where the city's true heart waits–
forgotten, abandoned, yearning?

Rinsed in coloured light
I watch myself dissolve in endless reflections,
each night peeling away another layer of who
I thought I was
everybody is looking for someone,
someone less melancholic
everyone is looking for someone
who understands without asking
With every finding, I keep looking for
something else,
my search never ends,
it always has a new beginning

For some of us, the present is nothing but an
endless echo of the past,
and the future–
never seems to arrive
living our childhood all through life
The city no longer has space for all, any more
it is running out of love

I have too much of spare time,
I see the world through the bottom of my
whisky glass;
a world goes out of fashion with every sunrise
the painting in the gallery is searching for a
home
children of broken homes
waking up to a different today,
the world is losing its mind
waking up to a different self every day
I am looking for me...

Pass it on... (for my son Ridhaan)

I

tell him,
more important than revolution and progress
is the moment,
everyone laments lost time
celebrate your moments

to be rich,
open your heart and accept the other
for only truth is infinite

to be creative,
open your mind and question the gods
for imagination is unbound

to be a wise,
transform yourself with the courage to learn
for in knowledge is the truth

tell him,

to love deeper and more fiercely with every
passing day,
endeavour to create a symphony and
not just be content with a song
of money being never enough
and that life can be deathless
only through the love we leave behind
in our deeds

tell him,
not tales of God or angels, but
of vision and perseverance that build Rome
and how all that crumbled into dust
under the weight of vanity and hubris

tell him,
no one wins in the end
no one loses
it's all balanced in a delicate equilibrium
upheld by the quiet, profound laws of life

tell him,
all that you know of life, love and longing
but for living
leave it unto him, to choose his own...

II

Spread out!
beyond time, beyond space–
spread as clarity amidst paradox,
as colours on an open canvas,
as emotions, as passion,
as unrequited desire,
as fear, as shame.

Spread through the folklore,
in belief and disbelief alike,
spread wide and thick,
in aspirations, inspirations,
in dreams, in death,
in rebirth and return.
Spread in creation,
and just as deeply, in destruction.

spread out
as poetry unto infinity
to contain the whole of life in you
and then stand united in its truth

as eternity becomes your root

only me

me
the
modern man
rose from humble origins into
complete disaster
living in an age of intense human action,
turbulent and lonely
leading to a silence secured only with
end of thoughts
my thoughts are born out of
wild internal disorders
my mind is the epicentre of
inflamed consciousness
and extravagant thoughts, its raging ideas
set me up for purposeless journeys
goaded by narcissism
and the impotency of privacy,

a neoteric privilege, which like
every circle of privilege is defined by
what it excludes
and everyday outlines its own
geometry of exclusion

I am
no longer an individual
but an affiliate of the virtual
woven through endless webs
cybernetic networks and communities
with proliferating connections
and discounted sagacity

I wander around the world with my valise
full of updates and breaking news
moving forward and backward in times
shifting indifferently through old patterns
as a failed husband and an uncertain lover
I am the hero of heartbreaks
frenzied by what it means
to be in love amid the clasp of technology
no one seems to know
what's that muddle all about!

as I peer beyond myself
like poetry, you come in different ways
shielding all my imperfections
with discounted expectations
at my best, I am a man of heart
and let the wisdom of hardened veins warn
you
least you think being that is easy
when love is made out of funeral pyre
it seems much more real that we shall only
meet in death
the black white and grey transform the world
in a way that
me and you can only talk in coded silence
about the time
I did a cameo in your dreams
from then on, every drop of tears reminds me
of you and
love comes back among betrayals
keeping the candles burning
and the flames
they know
love doesn't exist in itself
but only in the ambience of life

Tonight,
amidst the shame and hollow praise,
I descend into this body–
no words, no sound,
just raw, bald lechery erasing all else.
Dignity, decorum, pretension, vanity–
all stripped away,
until there is nothing.
No armour, no family, no god.
Just me,
standing alone in colossal ignorance.
me
Only
me

Sometimes

Sometimes, a smile comes without reason.
Sometimes, we crave to do nothing,
and sometimes, everything.
Sometimes, life endures the shadow of death.
Sometimes, there are only thorns, no roses.
Sometimes, even facts can lie.
Sometimes, we bleed even in our triumphs.
Sometimes, expression says it all,
Sometimes, words mean nothing
Sometimes, life blooms in abattoir
Sometimes, all the life around makes the city
so senile
Sometimes, words just don't come out right

Sometimes, we reveal more in our attempts to conceal
Sometimes, we hate as much as we love.

Portrait of a city stroll...

From where the city stands, life is just a flux
in time
nothing has changed beyond the surface –
fashion, slang
someone made it big; someone got raped
mob frenzied by fear sets the city on fire
obscure little faces of hope
rising prices everywhere
another impotent husband shadows
a slutty wife
and TV clowns make us laugh at
our own despair
the city neither nourishes nor heals
and life just passes by
unnoticed and unheeded.

Courage flickering sometimes
lights a fire
no one touches it
nothing burns
just a few flames
here and there

touched by the passion, the city singes
Dylan is singing in the neighbourhood
his opiated voice reminds me
of ganja-cigarettes and nauseous capsules
the city gets drunk several times a day
forever recuperating from the shadows
it has created

The city defies traditions
through resistance born out of
silent revulsions and anguish,
children of dead fathers,
yellow fire everywhere,
consuming all that was life;
the mighty establishments
stand in silence
and rapture

People endure it all,
dynasties, despots and destructions
people, ordinary people, everyday people,
define their time, capturing every changing
expression of time
in emotions
in words

in fear
in ignorance,
in poetry
and in love

Slowing down among weathered laurels,
beaten blue by the ravages of time;
holding on to old dogmas and history of grief
old families descended into decadence;
their grand mansions standing as
hollow relics,
abandoned to the nocturnal
horrors of silence.
turning into places where
flowers and poetry rust

All desires find their way with a little courage
Greed, the city's new muse, whispers in every
ear:
We want it all, and we want it now.
huge glass offices standing tall
they look like success drenched in
its own suffering

the city grows every day
with green death

Artisans of terror are taking over the city
weaving hatred with careful words
to incite our belligerent identities
every street reeks of malice,
every corner stained with blood
amongst all these
unabashed laughter melts my heart
people, despite it all, fall hopelessly in love
there's still
freedom to sing
to laugh
and there is
a little time for everything
remember me with 'Whatever yours is mine'
wished the city

The city talks
but we listen only to private interpretation
at twenty, looking for friends and assurances
she committed suicide
and the media reduced her to
anxiety and her blue panties

she was important to the city
but then death has always been more
important to life
from her eyes, death smiles back,
a twisted, sinister smile
we all sell for benefits; everyone's a whore
there is no privacy anymore and that,
                              sets us free
and god!
fucking dies every moment in this city
as rapists and murderers
roam free

In one such celebrated
chaotic hour,
the city pauses–
halts everything,
and simply watches
the rain
from where the city stands,
yesterday looks nothing like tomorrow
and it knows with a quiet certainty
that time will take it all,
Our pride,
our pain,

and, in the end,
us

Fear

There is a freedom in every renege
there is an agony laced within every ecstasy
there is hidden pain in every smile
there is a truth buried deep in every lie
the world torn apart into
the known and unknown
a thin line in between,
call it fear,
the fear of the unknown.

Coming Back to My Life

My repentances mourned
in the silence of my dreams
when you walked in like autumn breeze
as if the doors and windows
have been left ajar,
waiting just for you
and with you came memories of
dark and desperate times

A woman in her forties, desperately
calm and carefree,
returns once more to
the wilderness within.
Even back then, love was never innocent–
it carried the weight of macho insecurities
and feminine deceit,
a dance of desires wrapped
in layers of quiet deception.

release me from yourself
I, a man of sin
is frail as smoke today and

have burnt my fist of steel,
the purple wounds echo in
my inner void
I have aged in silence but
you have been there all through
as life went about consuming itself in
many come and go
my shadows reminded
of you

Intimate Conversations...

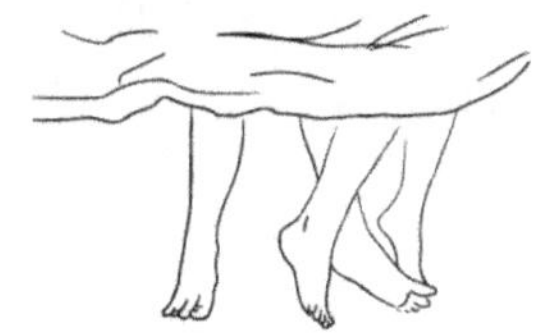

I

Stay in a silence that's only mine
Stay there alone
With me

II

'Stay with me,' she softly pled,
'I will bring you joy
in tender threads,
with kisses
so that you wake up
in love's embrace,
drowned by its depth,
lost in its grace'

III

all I have is this moment
where everything I touch, I do,
Is carrying me back to you

IV

In silence, my heart speaks to memories,
And I begin the journey back–
To places where I've once belonged,
Where fragments of me still quietly reside.
I go to meet them once again,
In the warmth of new light,
And the softness of new love

V

That smile
is your way into my heart
Where all my resistance softly ebbs,
Like unwritten laws that quietly
Defeat the ones carved in stone
love is the fire that feeds you

yet it's the flame
That burns me

VI

You've been crying in silence,
Amongst the fading stars,
Blue tears soaked deep
all the darkness of our fears.
I wander through the endless maze
of life's why's and how's,
yet love quietly bloomed
in the creaks and crevices
of our everyday.

VII

be a poet, she said once
and drift in verses
of defiance
and disturbance
of passion
and grief
be a poet, she said once
and bleed in words

that go down in whisky
and come up in smoke
be a poet of the soul
and rise above your own
love and hate
be a poet, she said once
of simplicity
and ignored realities
of forgotten words
and illusionary love
be a poet, she said once
of long isolations
and pale green hope

VIII

the night of love in its exuberance
of tranquil impatience hasten
the moment of desire
now, now is the hour
when we will perish in the magic
entangled in your loosened hair
I glide deep into you, exploring
the track breaking into life
we lay in intimate embrace

crowning into the moment of release
a gush of invigorating tidal elixir
cherished like the poet's tears
enthralled, we retire
but my heart remains open
for you to come in
anytime

HOPE

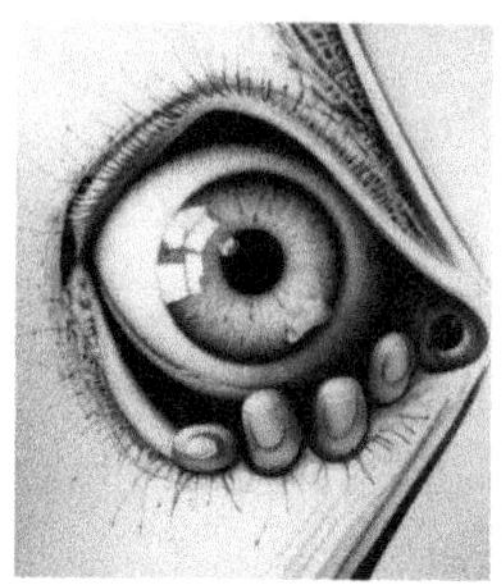

The dreamer comes out of his dreams
     Cold atrophy, colourless dreams
Walking along the uneven streets
     Strangers in bed, no time to decide,
abundance of lust
Known faces come out of the moon,
     No one remembers me anymore
We were friends long back in the city of light
     Behind all the facades, there is fear
I summon the death of poetry tonight
     Are you crying? Love.
Crying?
This is just the beginning, birth of tragedy
     On the roads of life
On the roads of life
     The sun shines low on the lizard king

I have been waking up for years on the other
side of the life, every night
                My dangers are many
my shadow stretches larger than me
                We are getting used to images
I am guilty of nothing
                I find solace in blood
Take the pill to kill, the conspiracy to kill a
child even before she is born
                Tribal dancers in grotesque masks
are coming towards my city
It's impossible to tell how many are there
                Seems like a lonely crowd,
unflinching zeal to be alive
Stop! Stop! Shoot
                A million epitaphs written
Nugatory lives, broken promises, bullet
slumber.

Are you more flesh and blood than me?
The painting on the wall is crying... cruel cry
Imagination on fire; poetry of lust; whiskey in
my eyes; purple sight

My nights are spent in you... redolence of
touches
                      a desire,
                      a dream,
                      a vision; fading
A lifelong search for Kafkan delights
Every night the moon throws its cruel light
on me
We shall still love
the clouds, the rains, a country far away,
rivers of hate and memories of silence
               my inheritance is lost,
               my paramours have departed
Masturbating love, desire for flesh, scandalous
death.
               Watering the stems and leaves,
                              thirsty
roots

Do you know, I am running for a thousand
years?
I am running in the labyrinth of my city
        Brick to brick,
        stone to stone,

grass to grass
Searching for an identity in the rapidly
losing geographies

Running towards where the winds came from
        I try hard to learn,
        learn to forget
The gentle breezy touch in the midst of May
The azure sky of my dreamy eyes
Learning to forget suicidal veins
In every pain
        I feel I exist
            In every joy the same
                I cannot differentiate
between the two;
they both whisper

I am alive.

No one comes in unless the city beckons
The blue light is spreading across our lives
Everything expands, infinity growing bigger
with every passing day
                Somebody

a poet,
a nobody,
comes down from the sky every night into the
island of earthly urge
Throw away the watches that keep ticking
away time
I want eternity
outside time,
freezing moments in the flow of infinity
I want time as it is, endless and pure
I am a rapporteur of all the
unnoticed moments of time

Love unwritten, in abundance, flowing
around
Let's take time from our sunrise marathon
to pick up pieces of love
For you, for me
My wild love is waiting for you in the depot,
they keep looking for you
and you for your own suffering
I don't mind waiting for you,
I am dead already
The night is just too long

I can let you go
I can let you go – again
Bathing in the blue light of my city,
I drift into eternity,
the ever-expanding eternity

All the questions that I once asked
never had an answer
But, you sat through your years of education
patiently looking for one
An academic answer for
questions of no answer
Left alone, I could never understand any
painting
Endless colours and disfigured females of
naked delight
   Fleshes of reflection,
   flashes of light
The eyes, every night
The kisses, every night
   Have you ever seen God?
He only smiles
   The radiant life calls us all
   The naked life calls us all

The ancient life calls us all
Hard dreams, soft light, unknown music
Open your eyes, see the children of death are
talking to the children of life
I never read poetry before,
I had a vision.

Life like it always is,
                changing
A new sun at every dawn,
                old eyes
All of us are fond of results;
time kills all the moments that form
memories
Life like it always was,
                changing
Open the doors to my memories of freedom
        Let it come back;
        Let it come back
To me, to us, memories of freedom, a missing
link

How do you punish yourself?
Why do you punish life?

I am walking to reach the other
side
Feel the universe functioning,
it's beautiful
Nothing can destroy life
All along, all through,
it just passes

Hope is all we have against the end–
Eyes of hope giving birth to
you
and
me.
Hope for the new, every dawn
Fear of the new, each night.
She told my mother, 'So long as your son
lives, he can never be free.'
And he paused, then added, 'So be it for all.'
from then on began the hope of freedom–
The endless hope of being alive in life.
I dwell in the unconscious, all the time,
Yet in every dream, I am awake.

Do you know what hurts the most?
Do you?

Do you?

I have hope, the hope of a life.
Come, join hands with me–
Let's march forward into time.
Between solitude and multitude,
I choose both,
one layered within the other.
Is there not enough earth for us all?
As you face the light,
I'm busy conjuring rain for you,
Our own private rain.
You are beautiful,
You and life.
Tonight, the moon brims with light.
We have to try; a golden generation is
waiting,
Waiting for us to try.
It should rain tonight,
rain, water, rain
forever we walk through our infinite roads of
freedom
planting hopes for
a wiser posterity.

Her Eyes

I looked into her eyes,
my sight piercing them
in search of the untold;
have you ever tasted tears,
It's like swallowing your pain.
I turned away and looked again,
behind the great torment of an abortive lie,
were a thousand roses in bloom.
Behind her eyes, behind her eyes
so deep, so lonely inside
was a lady unknown, was a speech without
words;
resplendence of love in the darkest of the
dark
Behind her eyes, behind her eyes
she was sitting by herself
groping her corpse in search of life.

I

I

I
and you
are all made of the many
yet
I am born out of me
nature is all that it is
beauty unfolds only in human stare
life smiles in delight
when in your own light
you unseal your lips
and unveil your eyes
to see who stands in siege
it always our

I

2

I
am a stillborn
who moves
only for money
and
slowly debased by time
turned into different caricatures of pity
looking to inflict pain
upon souls
tender than
mine

3

I am the open sky;
I am the cage
of all my imaginations...
I am the promise
I am the restraint
of all my dreams...
I am the father

I am the murder
of my own little desires...

4

I
exist in compartments
   glued together
       from here and there
               everywhere
from places I have never been
from people I have never met
I collected light of the unknown lands
and stored emptiness inside my childhood
home...

living as I know it
  is turning into a perennial separation
one cell at a time
one memory after another
        I am all that's left of time and space
so everybody from everywhere comes and
            meets into me

when the stars fade

and we are alone
come to meet me then
           there is a strange freedom in
darkness
a depth no light can reveal,
           and then I will show you sunrise
                only if you care enough to look
deeply
                into sunset

all my experience crystallises
           in this moment
as I touch you
           my hands tremble
but the dust is still heavy
                on my soul
all my poetry remains trapped
                in this moment
restless, I roll out
                into the waves
I run into the storm
           and there I feel
                my vastness
                my open space
and I know for sure

that all the myriad parts
come together in a beautiful whole
            that is

            me

...heartaches from a melancholy afternoon

1.0

a melancholy afternoon,
an afternoon heavy with loneliness.
I sit, lost in memories,
the past images slowly dissolving
into tears.
every breath, every motion,
feels like an attempt
to drag forward,
even as my heart pulls back
into the shadows of what once was.

But in the end,
no matter how much is lost,
I cannot lose myself.
Even when everything else fades,
I cling to the last fragments
of who I am,
alone,
but unbroken.

1.1
in the end
I sat there alone
poking a burnt-out fire
stirring embers, looking for my burnt beliefs
looking for stories I tell myself
in solitude
and in memories
of all things I call mine
the bravest are my dreams
all they need is Shaggy singing – the morning
is on its way
a reminder, an assurance
that life gives us way more
than it takes...

1.2
I finally go to sleep
with my head buzzing,
I leave the window open,
waiting for the icy wind of the dead
to slip inside.
I hear it whispering in my ears,
a sound only I can know,
a coldness that settles deep
in my bones.
The icy wind of the dead–
I feel its shame,
its silent, suffocating shame,
and I burst into tears,
It is impossible to close my eyes,
to find any rest
with her leftovers scattered all over me,

1.3
I am endlessly spinning
in circles of life and death,
each day another turn
in a spiral I can't escape.
as I trudge through life,
everything I name 'life'

seems to orbit around death.
we die in love,
and then love dies–
all the while,
I carry death
in the marrow
of my being–
my breath
my heartbeats

1.4
I remain hidden within myself,
a shadow lurking beneath my own skin.
Cigarettes dangle at the corner of my lips,
dragging my desperation
with every slow inhale,
consumed by the dullness
of my own boredom.
I know–
I must come around,
someday,
to settle the debts,
to pay for all the broken promises
I've scattered along the way,
But still, I delay,

postponing the day
I'll have to face what
I've left undone...

1.5
All I can remember
is the dust in the wind
a chorus of taunting whispers
and your assassin's glare.
I tried my best to forget
but they remained within me
Like a vague knot of memories

I find myself staring
at a bottomless vase,
its hollow centre holding
all my sunsets,
all the endings
I can never reclaim.

1.6
I can hear sounds
from a lost interval of time,
I close my eyes,
losing myself

in a long-ago darkness.
In that thick blackness,
a faint glow hovers,
a promise,
a possibility
I stretch out my hand,
yearning to touch it,
to pull it close,
but the glow
remains just beyond my grasp–

1.7
If you've ever lived through
a long, melancholy afternoon,
you'd know time doesn't fly
in a straight line.
Unlike the confused hands of a clock,
spinning endlessly on a single point,
time keeps circling back to you–
all you can do is wait,
quietly, patiently,
until the moment comes
when time finds you again and
you're ready to carry your
own light,

1.8
I kept watching the patterns
the raindrops formed on the window glass,
my attention swayed by the winds
of my restless heart.
I sat there alone,
trying hard to make sense of the silence
inside me.
The roots of darkness spread through my
body,
creeping patiently, taking their time
to reach every corner of me.
Memories wrap my empty heart.
I am withdrawing,
no sense of how long I will remain here,
waiting wordlessly...
1.9
Afternoon clouds drifted like desire,
stitched together by fading hope.
Raindrops bled into the soul of the
abandoned,
shivering with regret,
wrestling with memories–
like a horde of restless souls

in the midst of a distressful siesta.
I wake, barefoot, to find
life still embraces me,
despite it all.

2.0
entering slowly within me
one stratum at a time
the waiting lingers on
through an afternoon, busy
scattering solitude all over its skyline
I am lost
the impending sunset my only witness
I am wandering
among a labyrinth of roads that lead
nowhere
I am comforted
by the security of its melancholy embrace
I am wavering
Between the infinite yeses and noes
of my being,
learning, painfully slowly,
that not all roads lead back home

pondering...

I

gloom and gay
plays in a way
that nothing
is itself

we all stand in a place
where it started
even before life began on Earth
with the solemn promise
of the ballet of death

all the purging that happens
silently within
takes me to consciousness
and the first luminous fondle
incept the pondering
how much of 'who am I'
is driven by 'why am I'

II

'I saw the best minds of my generation'
fall like autumn leaves in an empty
orchestra room amongst scattered
manuscripts of
Ricardo, Ford, Carnegie and Smith
rotting in the rage of indifference
in a hallucinatory void
withering away like blank pages
dynamos they were once
cradled by the city, cherished by the sea
robed in power and tanned in glee
eyes set at the apex of affluence
they worked out the trails to treasure
but skies quivered in the darkness of the
mountain fumes and
it happened
all that was not to be
the torrid air peeled off their skin
the one they had built to make an impression
and were exalted in return
now rancid and bitter   soaked
in acid rain
bruised by the veiled impales

tired and covered in the rust of a life
where luxury is abundance
just not enough care
ready now to exchange an empire
for sleep, the all-humbling sleep
and in its quiet depth, ready to lose the world
at the heart of it all,
there isn't much–
just this simple truth:
they don't get enough love.

III

one with the mayhem;
one with the silence
one with the memories
one with the now
one with the anxieties;
one with the imagination
I touch myself

Happiness...

It's all just a chase, isn't it?
Happiness – a ghost in the fog,
A flicker you reach for
But can never hold.
We tell ourselves a story:
If life bends to our will,
We'll finally be whole.
But it doesn't, not often,
And the chase goes on.

Round and round,
A spinning wheel,
The faster you run,
The further it feels.

What if you stopped?
What if you stood still?
Right here, in this moment,
Not the one you wish for,
But the one that simply is.

Feel the quiet.
Hear the hum.
There's no promise here,
No grand design–
But there's truth.

Let the ghost fade.
Let the wheel turn without you.
In stillness, you'll find
The now is enough–
Wild, unbroken,
Beautifully whole.

To Night and Dawn

the night no longer speaks to me, quietly it
comes in
through the door
and kisses me with its cold unseen lips
but not a word
it's this stillness and not in words
that we talk

my flesh is melting
I live beyond this incomplete body
to the promisors of the Promised Land
I must ask
who decides reason?
whose reason stands?
is it the silence
or you
or everybody on their own?

the night no longer speaks to me
but I have started talking to the dawn
in the language of deeper silence

A Way to be Good Again...

I feel restrained
caught in a world that breathes hate
where every vision I cling to feels
trapped, shattered against the jagged edges of
life
A part of me remains blind, perpetually
lost, questioning the fragile assumptions of
self

perception is all I have
me is my love,
my hate,
my inhibitions,
my freedom
my mind is my universe

my mind keeps playing its games
dragging me through the shadows of
possibilities left undone
It whispers questions I can't escape,
a relentless echo of what if?

I am alive in the quiet yearning for a way back,
a path that whispers,
There's still a way to be good again

Of All That Wounds and
All That Heals

Of all my woes and fleeting bliss,
What part of me remains in this?
Each tear I've shed, each silent cry,
Has carved its mark; yet, who am I?

Seek not to veil what lies within,
For every virtue, every sin,
Is weighed by time's unyielding hand,
Its whispers are carved in shifting sand.

All is known, and all is judged,
Each fault forgiven; each scar begrudged.
Yet in the labyrinth time conceals,
All fades, dissolves and softly heals.

And still, the wheel begins anew,
The old made fresh, the false made true.
What's done is lost, then born again,
Through endless cycles of joy and pain.

So why pretend, why seek to flee,

When all I am is only me...
The stars may watch, the heavens wait,
But I am both my love and my hate.

So, linger not in vain regret,
For time erases and resets.
We are but echoes, bound to roam,
Until the stars reclaim us home.
And thus, we turn
again, again
through joy,
through sorrow,
through love,
through pain.

Last Game

Pensive blue
stretches across my morning sky,
a quiet canvas of longing.
Yellow creeps in,
the melancholy haze of obscured afternoons,
where shadows linger longer than light.

Evenings press their violet weight upon my
heart,
a gentle suffocation of gloom.
And night, restless and variegated,
spills across the streets like a silent tide,
its edges blurred with secrets.

Whisky on ice,
bitter on my tongue.
there's blood in my eyes,
red and raw,
a reflection of battles fought,
and lost

So, ready?

for the last game of chess
with life?

Murmurs of a senile mind...

Time, pleated like a crisply ironed shirt,
is abandoned now,
folded into some pallid corner of memory.
I've grown a taste for suffering–
bitter, familiar and mine alone.
I've never questioned it:
the why, the how or even
when it will end.
Instead, I drift from year to year,
scorched beneath an indifferent sun,
my voice lost in the cacophony,
a whisper I no longer recognise.
For a time, we had each other,
a fragile tether to fill the hollow of our
breath.
But even that feels distant now,
a shadow of what was never meant to last.
I envy those who left too soon,
who never had to carry the ghost of human
future–
our future that slips through the grasp,

more and more every day
anyways, all it is but
meaningless in the face of time's indifference

The Waiting

I am waiting,
amid the relics of all that was,
beneath the frigid ridges,
amongst the blistering barrens of time.

I am waiting,
for myself in this endless wait for you,
hoping that this pause might pull us
from the fragments of our daily triviality,
bring us back from the edges of what we've
forgotten.

Waiting alone,
vanquished by the weight of ennui,
sun-stripped, exposed,
waiting for my wait to end.

I am old now,
older than love itself,
the music no longer plays,
and words are slowly slipping into silence.
All that remains is

Just waiting...

A City Impasse

A city standstill;   cacophony of
interest
            Broken window panes, buses set
ablaze
Patches of blood,
        here and there; livid emotions...

Empty 303 cartridges glint in the dust,
lifeless bodies on the road
Mutilated pennons,
        scattered pamphlets.
                    pulverised identities
Hope of a better destiny;
the eternal mirage of free will...

An abandoned slipper;
a lonesome world
Angry words;
reneged promises
Empty cigarette cases;   disquieted
silence...

A crowd on both sides,
mirror images of each other,
no faces
no individuals
just renounced hearts
A moment of sudden emergence;
end of tolerance
Memories of unfulfilled dreams;
deceased friends
The desire for a promised land;
delusion of equality

Between them, there lie years of rape,
carnage, murder, slavery, hatred and blood,
There is no empty space left...

In their veins   vengeance,
In their minds   fear
In their words   hatred
In their hearts   suspicion
In their intent   greed

Time teaches everyone their right to be
human,
Up against the law

Up against the authority
Up against the injustice

One stands against the other
                        Man against Man
One reality against another
                        Ideology against
reality
Perception against perception
                        Promised land
against Promised Land

                        No matter
who wins
                power has its own code

                and violence has been the
catalyst for change
and will be once more!!

Oh! Kolkata...

oh Kolkata!!
a hymn of chaos, a flawless
symphony of errors and disasters
played out to perfection by people
wearing painted faces
a defiant disregard for the sanctity of
another's truth,
the cacophony of dissent
which became its own flawed symphony
over generations

sanity in tatters,
accusation and violence left us shattered,
as paranoia seeps through the city and
the delicate
veil of rationality slips,
there are no individuals left,
everyone puzzled at what they have become
clones and colours

oh Kolkata!!
we have laughed and talked,

we listened until salvos broke the silence
and ideology stole our voices,
you taught us what does it means
to believe in something,
When the world is tearing itself apart?

in retrospect,
it feels like death was always the muse,
everything else – just a fleeting pretext,
people smiled, debated the fusion of
cuisines,
chased illusions of purpose in borrowed
ideals
yet beneath it all, they waited,
silent and still,
for death to arrive.
the only certainty in a world of pretences

oh Kolkata!!
living through the mysterious succession
of joy and grief,
of affairs and protests
of lovemaking and fears
and a residue of undone dreams

lingering like shadows on the
walls of memory
everything unfinished, every essence lost

thank you
for the rains, the stirring rains
clogging the
gateways to the rusty bars
and covering the
city
in a diaphanous veil
which covers virtually
nothing of your nakedness.
yet it whispers truths we'd rather not know
creating illusions which lure us to embrace
shadows as friends

oh Kolkata!!
love slowly entrapped us in a series of
lies and pretences
all that is human is but a perspective
and every generation has its own
propaganda mellowed the howling of hunger,
everything a cut-paste from everywhere,

the ignominy of having fallen behind in all
domains,
and finally
the government fell

oh Kolkata!!
with age, your shadows seem more
threatening, their games more predictable
and playing it feels dreary, now that
my friends are all gone

thank you
for the many moments laced with
whisky
and words,
life and experience
beyond the realm of moral
creeds,
many altercations
aside, we did not
end up as strangers
to each other,
so before I stealthily dissolve into
you,
let us for the last time

kiss goodbye
as lovers

Jazz only night

Jazz only night
it was at my beloved jazz club
Jazz helps me walk into the timeless sadness
of existence
Where, in spite of our best efforts, no one
matches up in the end
Another glass down, my eyes are now red
　　With lust and haze

And it was then
that she walked in...

She walked in like a murderer in her dazzling
evening gown,
She walked with a grace, lightening a smile

as she passes them
She came straight to the bar table,
two quick shots of vodka
and a dangling cigarette on her bloody red
lips,

And then she opened her mask and kept it on
the table
Lets her hair go wild;
her face turned tender and soulful... now she
was ready,
Ready to publish her own scandal,
ready to lose herself in the whirlwind of
dancing and frenzy...
she looked straight into my eyes and asked
'Light the fire'

The moment she walked in, I knew she was an
interruption
To the Jazz only Night
her music had a reckless rhythm, rusty and
tranquil
there was fire in all corners of her body
carried with a careless demeanour...
she carried the weight of a love so deep, it left
her lonely.
Terribly, terribly lonely.

suddenly she stopped talking...
touched my palms and told me, tell me a
story...

which story, I enquired...
that story, she said, the one you have not told
anyone,
the one which is important, eternal and
sacred to you,
the one which whispers in your blood,
the one who's lost paradise continues to linger
in every fibre of your damaged soul,
tell me that story

from that moment, I loved her with all my
vigour
I hated her equally powerfully,
she was the perfect stranger laced with
tainted grace
and that made her someone
to whom you could open the
deepest crevices of your heart
for one thing people like me know, by people
like me, I mean the ones who keep
secrets in their hearts...
that you become terribly lonely when you
keep secrets

I started talking

a feeling of relief and joy washed all over me...
I kept talking and talking, like a muted
television which has got its sound back
We looked at each other and kept staring
Lost in our thoughts, wanting the moment to
stop questioning
Our inhibitions
And jump into the reality of our bodies...

A Passing Affair

They live their love,
in the strange attraction of eyebrows
that tickled down their eyes
making them feel like
the dead tired sun
burnt alive, in the radiance of
forbidden desire

They live their love,
by stealing million moments,
of freedom
from lives
regimented by corporate dreams

They live their love,
in the sky where spirits live,

staring at the eternal blue
listening to the whistling palms
and telling their story
to answer questions
never asked

They live their love,
in painting the memories of a city
lived in auto rides,
she knew the city too well
and he knew her moods
between all the madness,
the city was touched for
the first time

They live their love,
in their sin, beyond themselves
in the silence of unspoken emotions,
in the forgotten alleys
of a deserted city,
flooded by rain;
November rain

They live their love,
in places where a few go on their own

where love can be experienced every moment
by burning yourself alive
and every joy comes at the expense of
your familiar life

They live their love,
in looking for a social name for their relation,
searching for a structure,
a witness,
who would understand
and all they could find was their longing
drenched in tears,
they looked back at love
with love again

They live their love,
intoxicated every night
chasing the unknown,
holding each other
and searching for the pulse,
in between the bodies
they touched their soul

They live their love,
in places where all love ends,

riding through the city looking for
words to describe the smell
and in whispers they realised
that all leads to nothing
and true bliss is in nothingness

They live their love,
for hours kissing,
cuddling and staring at each other,
wondering if the neighbours know,
and in their shared disappointment,
was the taste of their desire

They live their love,
in the idea of love and when it touched
reality,
all that was left was shadows
and the possibility of what could have been;
they lived their love
on the other side of life

They live their love,
in half-written deaths
scavenging pieces of life from wherever they
could find some,

going around the world measuring distance
between the places in plastic scales
and in the end, all they could find was their
way back home

They live their love,
in the dance of erotic freedom in a city,
falling apart in the night-time blues,
the distant images still alive in some
unknown part of the city
waiting for the promised walk,
the walk under the red sun

They live their love,
in talks of other men and women,
moments spent in realisation of their absence
of wings,
the inability to move away from what has
been
and in the process discovering
how strange they were
a little crazy perhaps,
one stranger than the other

They live their love,

in alcoholic fumes reciting Elliot at the top of
their voice,
occupied in discussions about the 'time past
and time future'
and from the steel silence of their
conversations,
discovered that it's only in the 'time present'
that the shadow falls;
asking for
an answer

They live their love,
writing colours of rainbow in the halogen
lights
deeply absorbed in thoughts,
wondering if rainbows are actually
the stairway to heaven
and then frantically calling to discuss their
new discovery
with friends from the city
they called home

They live their love,
in travelling through three cities

on the same day discovering the multiplicity
of self,
by mesmerising a car full of audience by
narrating stories with glimpses of truth
and from the funeral debri of
their own ego self found the courage
to stand up for love

They live their love,
in a place called dream,
with reality touching every changing
expression on their face
and searching places for their quick sexual
wanting,
oblivious to the world around
looking desperately for sleep

They live their love,
travelling endlessly through time
dozing in their workstations
and staying awake all night,
making hasty decisions
and fighting the limitations of human
physical endurance
to live a dream which felt more real

only in each other's arms

They live their love,
in dingy pubs, drinking beer
with the music loud and lights dimmed
bringing the purple out of the haze
around by throwing flames in the fire
fighting destiny with eyes fixed on each other
till the music got over
and they turned
on the lights

They live their love,
in two sets of emotions
examining every feeling for the value they
expressed,
their mind kept moving restlessly from,
one possibility to another
their lips trembling in the guilt of their
emotions,
everything moving; one faster than the other
every second dynamic,
the only thing constant
being the desire of their heart

They live their love,
in relativity,
struggling through their personal truth
to discover the absolute truth of the universe;
they realised,
that in order to live love,
there can't be any rules,
human heart is a
free zone

They live their love,
smoking cigarettes,
every drag a reminder of their mortality,
each drag
a passing moment,
a passing thought,
a passing life,
and before they could really make sense of it,
a passing affair
became life

you and me

I

Your purity unveiled my filth,
and no length of time can make me forget
Your love was always
greater than my malice
in a room littered with distrust
your face illuminated in its
youthful air turns into a feeling
that I recollect
as love
a tender smile
rare, just like an embryo
coming to life
your feet brushed against time
and your smile is all I hold–
in illusions
in realities

II

Amid the interruptions of silence,

Where the woods whistle softly,
I roam all night with your shadow,
Adding your existence to my madness.
from the time I have known women
I have not lived without loving
but to my naked heart
you are the one
a friend, a lover, muse of men
who taught me how to repent
not in blood or tears
but in action

From cigarette-smoking hipsters,
We've grown over years
Into a single face
all of our love can be explained by this
I think about you
and smile
But still, the question lingers:
Do we love each other,
Or the image we hold of the other?

III

you and I lived a life

in the numerous manipulations of love
in the pleasures of flesh
in the malady of romance
we lived in the city lanes,
in the mofussil and in the countryside
beyond good and evil
together in a single verse
but, was it ours
or did we borrow one?

IV

amongst all my hatred
dislike, complain and angst
I discover you
your pain
    your tears
        your inestimable sadness

after every rift, I realise
you in my numberless infinite
maybe in matters of life
opposites are most alike

you played the piano keys and

while I groped for the symphony
plagued by lust and envy
my soul turned blue
and in a life without you
winds and women come and go
without knowing who
was Michelangelo…

V

In you,
I have spent the last love of this world,
Until none was left,
Only empty, vagrant expressions.
You were exacting; I, amenable–
by all measures what
a miracle we were
but nowhere in the universe
I can swear
can you find love
perfectly true and fair

finally, we sat down to discuss reasons for
love's quiet death
and in the crematorium

I finally opened myself to
the joy of the way the world lives
there is no meaning to life but
in living
we moved in circles from
one crematorium to another,
where we planted our soul yesterday
is covered with grass now
eyes fixed on the funeral pyre
I stood to release all memory,
To lean into the unknown and leap.
And from that moment, I became a man
with no past.

my grace, my art, my pleasures
are like yesterday's smoke
I daren't anymore
turn that way

VI

In the end, you and I shall fade,
Disappearing into legend without a trace–
to unite in
the tender harmony of death,

and in our union,
Death shall no longer be death,
but a gentle slumber,
before we wake up
Into eternity.

All that was left...

All that was left by my bedside was
indifference.
Loads of it – piled up like old books no one
reads.
Some of it came from faraway places,
Like postcards from strangers who never
meant to write.
Some of it came from people I thought I
knew,
Some of it came from the silence I was
seeking
The kind of silence that feels heavier than
words.
And the rest?
Well, the rest was mine – my own,
Born somewhere deep where even I don't go
often.
It felt like that orange autumn glow,
You know the one – soft, almost tender,

It just... hangs there,
Beautiful and hollow all at once.

I wondered what it wanted from me.
Was it a lesson?
Or a warning?
Or just the way things are sometimes?
I reached out to touch it once,
But it slipped away like water through my
fingers.
And maybe that's the point—
It's there for me, but never really mine.